Life's Little Inspiration Book
timeless wisdom for everyday living

by the author of *Footprints*

MARGARET FISHBACK POWERS

HarperCollins*PublishersLtd*

To Dr Geoffrey and Beverly Still, my true friends.

The Scripture quotations in this book are taken
from the Authorised King James Version, and
the New Revised Standard Version Bible,
copyright © 1989 by the Division of Christian
Education of the National Council of the
Churches of Christ in the USA. Used by
permission. All rights reserved.

First published in the U.K. by Marshall Pickering,
an Imprint of HarperCollins Religious, part of
HarperCollins Publishers: 1995

First Canadian edition: 1995

Canadian Cataloguing in Publication Data

Powers, Margaret Fishback
  Life's little inspiration book

ISBN 0-00-638038-7

1. Devotional literature, Canadian (English).*
I. Title.

BV4832.2.P68 1995   242   C95-930183-6

95 96 97 98 99 RRD 10 9 8 7 6 5 4 3

Printed and bound in the United States

INTRODUCTION

Over the years, before I wrote the poem *Footprints* and ever since, my husband Paul and I have collected thousands of sayings, thoughts and quotes, hastily writing them down as they came to us – in our Bibles, in our diaries, in notebooks – even on paper napkins and the occasional doily! Many of them have come from Paul's sermons; he has a habit of coming up with some good 'one-liners', as he calls them.

The thoughts collected here have been written over many years and reflect not only the highs and lows of my life, but, I trust, God's unceasing faithfulness and goodness to all who trust in His saving grace.

Some of these lines came when I needed to laugh at myself, others when I was riding high on 'me' – just as a reminder of who put 'me' in the picture in the first place! Others came from our two daughters, and some from 'out of the mouths of babies' – new believers in the faith trying to express their trust and faith in Jesus Christ.

Many came as a result of hearing how God had used the *Footprints* poem to lift up lives in need of comfort, hope, promise, companionship or encouragement. Like the poem, these thoughts focus on one of God's greatest promises to us, 'I WILL NEVER LEAVE YOU'.

A friend of mine, Jody Bergsma, is an artist. She did the artwork for a small card we carry in our Bibles. It shows a mother and child walking along hand in hand. The caption reads, 'Parents hold their children's hand for a while...their hearts for ever'. This is the way it is with our relationship with the Lord. We may let go, but He keeps us in His heart for ever. And if, as we walk through life, we feel that God is not there, who has moved? Not God; He has promised, 'I WILL NEVER LEAVE YOU'.

To follow in the Lord's footsteps we need help, humour and humility. My prayer is that as you dip into this little book you will find encouragement for yourself and your loved ones, and something to share with those for whom life is an uphill struggle. Who would argue that this world needs plenty of comfort and cheer!

Margaret Fishback Powers
Author of the poem *Footprints* and the book *Footprints: the story behind the poem.*
British Columbia, Canada 1994

FOOTPRINTS

One night I dreamed a dream.
I was walking along the beach with my Lord.
Across the dark sky flashed scenes from my life.
For each scene, I noticed two sets of footprints in the sand,
one belonging to me and one to my Lord.
When the last scene of my life shot before me
I looked back at the footprints in the sand
and to my surprise,
I noticed that many times along the path of my life
there was only one set of footprints.
I realized that this was at the lowest
and saddest times of my life.
This always bothered me
and I questioned the Lord
about my dilemma.

'Lord, you told me when I decided to follow You,
You would walk and talk with me all the way.
But I'm aware that during the most troublesome
times of my life there is only one set of footprints.
I just don't understand why, when I needed You most,
You leave me.'
He whispered, 'My precious child,
I love you and will never leave you
never, ever, during your trials and testings.
When you saw only one set of footprints
it was then that I carried you.'

Written by Margaret Fishback Powers,
Thanksgiving, 1964.

Where the footprints of God lead you,
the grace of God can keep you.

*Blessed be the Lord, the God of Israel, who
alone does wondrous things.*

PSALM 72:18

The STOPS of a good man are ordered by the Lord as well as his STEPS. (G. Mueller)

The Lord is good to those who wait for him...

LAMENTATIONS 3:25

Unless we reach our children's hearts today,
they will break our hearts tomorrow.
(Paul L. Powers)

*Suffer the little children to come unto me, and forbid them
not: for of such is the kingdom of God.*

MARK 10:14 AV

The caves of sorrow have mines of diamonds.

Weeping may linger for the night, but joy comes with the morning.

PSALM 30:5B

The world's largest mission field begins
just outside your door.

...go and proclaim the kingdom of God.

LUKE 9:60B

Use your mistakes as a guidepost,
not a hitching post.

*If we confess our sins, he who is faithful and just
will forgive us our sins and cleanse us from
all unrighteousness.*

1 JOHN 1:9

Some people don't recognize opportunity
because it comes dressed in work clothes.

In all toil there is profit, but mere talk
leads only to poverty.

PROVERBS 14:23

'Do it NOW' is more than a motto:
it's a way of life.

*...See, now is the acceptable time; see, now is
the day of salvation!*

2 CORINTHIANS 6:2

Cheer up! The sun (Son) hasn't
gone out of business.

*Arise, shine; for thy light is come, and the glory
of the Lord is risen upon thee.*

ISAIAH 60:1 AV

Of all your worries, great or small, the
worst of them never happened at all.

*Do not worry about anything, but in everything by
prayer and supplication with thanksgiving let
your requests be made known to God.*

PHILIPPIANS 4:6

Worry gives a small thing a big shadow.

*And can any of you by worrying add a
single hour to your span of life?*

MATTHEW 6:27

Defeat isn't bitter if you don't swallow it.

*Put away from you all bitterness and wrath and anger
and wrangling and slander, together with all malice...*

EPHESIANS 4:31

He who has a sharp tongue
cuts his own throat.

*From the same mouth come blessing and cursing.
My brothers and sisters, this ought not to be so.*

JAMES 3:10

If you learn from losing, then you haven't lost.

A rebuke strikes deeper into a discerning person
than a hundred blows into a fool.

PROVERBS 17:10

The secret of spiritual advance is true
and complete openness to God.

...him that cometh to me I will in no wise cast out.

JOHN 6:37 AV

The only safe and sure way to destroy enemies
is to make them your friend.

*But I say to you that listen, Love your enemies,
do good to those who hate you...*

LUKE 6:27

A selfish heart desires love for itself.
A Christian heart delights to love –
without return.

Whoever does not love does not know
God, for God is love.

1 JOHN 4:8

Some people drink at the fountain of knowledge; others just gargle.

...Let anyone who is thirsty come to me, and let the one who believes in me drink.

JOHN 7:37,38

Forget your mistakes, but remember
what they taught you.

*And we know that all things work together for good to
them that love God, to them who are called
according to his purpose.*

ROMANS 8:28 AV

Many little things are of greater value than big
things. Could a cup of water
exist without each drop?

...if you have faith the size of a mustard seed...
nothing will be impossible for you.

MATTHEW 17:20

Experience is what is left over after
you make a mistake.

*When pride comes, then comes disgrace; but
wisdom is with the humble.*

PROVERBS 11:2

God formed us; sin deformed us; but Christ can transform us.

*For all have sinned, and come short of the glory of God;
being justified freely by his grace through the
redemption that is in Christ Jesus.*

ROMANS 3:23-24 AV

The God we worship writes His name
on our faces.

...you will make me full of gladness with your presence.

ACTS 2:28B

Today, did you put your faith to test or to rest?

*For I am not ashamed of the Gospel of Christ: for
it is the power of God unto salvation to
every one that believeth.*

ROMANS 1:16A AV

You can't dream yourself into a character;
you must forge yourself into one.

*...suffering produces endurance, and endurance produces
character, and character produces hope...*

Romans 5:3B-4

As soon as the soul ceases to grow,
the man is dead.

*To set the mind on the flesh is death, but to set the
mind on the Spirit is life and peace.*

ROMANS 8:6

Faith always takes the first step forward.

Now the Lord said to Abram, 'Go from your country and your kindred...to the land that I will show you...'. So Abram went, as the Lord had told him.

GENESIS 12:1,4A

Bitterness is like a boomerang; the
moment you fling it, it returns.

A soft answer turns away wrath, but a
harsh word stirs up anger.

PROVERBS 15:1

Never measure the mountain until you
have reached the top, then you
will see how low it is.

...the God who girded me with strength...
set me secure on the heights.

PSALM 18:32A,33B

God has great confidence in you to
place you where you are.

*Here am I, the servant of the Lord; let it
be with me according to your word.*

LUKE 1:38

We stop forgiving others, when
Christ stops forgiving us.

*And if the same person sins against you seven times a
day, and turns back to you seven times and says,
'I repent', you must forgive.*

LUKE 17:4

You will never win the world
with your spare cash.

*Honour the Lord with your substance...then
your barns will be filled with plenty.*

PROVERBS 3:9, 10

If we have pleasant thoughts, even when we are alone, we are in good company.

I remember the days of old, I think about all your deeds,
I meditate on the works of your hands.

PSALM 143:5

Thought is the soul's chariot, a thoughtless man
doesn't let his soul go anywhere.

You know when I sit down and when I rise up;
you discern my thoughts from far away.

PSALMS 139:2

The world is not a playground;
it is a schoolroom.

*So teach us to count our days that we
may gain a wise heart.*

PSALM 90:12

You can't break God's promises
by leaning on them.

What then are we to say was gained by Abraham...?
No distrust made him waver concerning the promise of
God, but he grew strong in his faith as
he gave glory to God.

ROMANS 4:1,20

If you find excuses for sin, your sin
will never be excused.

For I acknowledge my transgressions:
and my sin is ever before me.

PSALM 51:3 AV

Prepare and prevent instead of
repair and repent.

Therefore you also must be ready, for the Son of Man
is coming at an unexpected hour.

MATTHEW 24:44

More depends on will power than brain power.

Choose life...loving the Lord your God, obeying him, and holding fast to him; for that means life to you and length of days...

DEUTERONOMY 30:19B, 20A

They greatly dare who greatly trust.

So Daniel was taken up out of the den, and no kind of harm was found on him, because he had trusted in God.

DANIEL 6:23B

If our faith were greater, our
deeds would be larger.

*Whatever you ask for in prayer with
faith, you will receive.*

MATTHEW 21:22

I am responsible to God for the talent
He has given me.

*...to one he gave five talents, to another two, to
another one, to each according to his ability...*

MATTHEW 25:15

A man who goes through life looking for a
soft thing can find it under his hat.

*The appetite of the lazy craves, and gets nothing, while
the appetite of the diligent is richly supplied.*

PROVERBS 13:4

To take care of oneself is the first law of nature,
but to deny oneself is the
first law of grace.

*If any want to become my followers, let them deny
themselves and take up their cross and follow me.*

MARK 8:34

Educate children without faith, and you make a
race of clever devils.
(Duke of Wellington)

*Train children in the right way, and when
old, they will not stray.*

PROVERBS 22:6

Think less about your rights and
more about your duties.

Do not be deceived...for you reap whatever you sow.

GALATIANS 6:7

Conversion to Christ makes useful
saints out of useless sinners.

*So if anyone is in Christ, there is a new creation:
everything old has passed away.*

2 CORINTHIANS 5:17

The glory of God is a man fully alive.
(Irenaeus)

You see that faith was active along with (Abraham's) works, and faith was brought to completion by the works...and he was called the friend of God.

JAMES 2:22, 23

Trouble starts when we become our brother's
keeper and cease to be his friend.

*Let each of you look not to your own interests, but to the
interests of others. Let the same mind be in you
that was in Christ Jesus...*

PHILIPPIANS 2:4-5

The final test of faith is not how much you
believe, but how much you love.

*You shall love the Lord your God with all your heart,
and with all your soul, and with all your
strength, and with all your mind.*

LUKE 10:27

Wherever the Spirit of the Lord sways a heart, there is a passion to serve.

...let us consider how to provoke one another to love and good deeds.

HEBREWS 10:24

No smile is so beautiful as the one
that struggles through tears.

He will yet fill your mouth with laughter,
and your lips with shouts of joy.

JOB 8:21

With every rising of the sun, think
of your life as just begun.

The steadfast love of the Lord never ceases, his mercies
never come to an end; they are new every morning.

LAMENTATIONS 3:22-23

It is better to forgive and forget
than to resent and remember.

...forgive us our debts, as we forgive our debtors.

Matthew 6:12 AV

The tongue being in a wet place, slippeth.
(Paul L.Powers)

...the tongue is a small member, yet it boasts of great exploits. How great a forest is set ablaze by a small fire!

JAMES 3:5

As you think, so you are; you
make or mar your success.

*...whatsoever things are true, whatsoever things are
honest, whatsoever things are just, whatsoever things are
pure, whatsoever things are lovely, whatsoever
things are of good report...think on these things.*

PHILIPPIANS 4:8 AV

With the last step of the race you
cross the finishing line.

...let him that thinketh he standeth take heed lest he fall.

1 CORINTHIANS 10:12 AV

Being faithful on the job beats carrying
a rabbit's foot for luck.

*Many proclaim themselves loyal, but who
can find one worthy of trust?*

PROVERBS 20:6

The soul would have no rainbow if
the eyes had no tears.

*O that my head were a spring of water,
and my eyes a fountain of tears...*

JEREMIAH 9:1A

Great souls have wills; feeble
ones only wishes.

*I am coming soon; hold fast to what you have,
so that no one may seize your crown.*

REVELATION 3:11

Count the day lost, when you
have done no worthy deed.

*What good is it, my brothers and sisters, if you say you
have faith but do not have works?*

JAMES 2:14

Call on God for help, but row
away from the rocks.

*When the righteous cry for help, the Lord hears,
and rescues them from all their troubles.*

PSALM 34:17

Some tread lightly through life,
others crush the flowers.

Let your gentleness be known to everyone.

PHILIPPIANS 4:5

A child is likely to see God as Father,
if they see God in their father.

...the glory of children is their parents.

PROVERBS 17:6B

No work in the world pays like mother's work.

Then he went down with them and came to Nazareth, and was obedient to them. His mother treasured all these things in her heart.

LUKE 2:51

God sees tomorrow more clearly
than we see yesterday.

He calls his own sheep by name...he goes ahead of them,
and the sheep follow him because they know his voice.

JOHN 10:3,4

A true friend is like the shade of a
great tree in the noonday heat.

*A friend loves at all times, and kinsfolk
are born to share adversity.*

PROVERBS 17:17

It's easier to pick a wise man by
the things he doesn't say.

One who spares words is knowledgeable.

PROVERBS 17:27A

The lazier we are today, the more
we have to do tomorrow.

The way of the lazy is overgrown with thorns.

PROVERBS 15:19A

The truest expression of Christianity
is not a sigh, but a song.

*Let the word of Christ dwell in you richly...and with
gratitude in your hearts sing psalms, hymns,
and spiritual songs to God.*

COLOSSIANS 3:16

The beginning is half of the whole.

...the one who began a good work among you will bring it to completion by the day of Jesus Christ.

PHILIPPIANS 1:6

When life writes 'Ended', the
angels write 'Begun'.

Those who believe in me, even though they die, will live.

JOHN 11:25B

Songs are heartbursts of gladness.

For this I will extol you, O Lord, among the nations, and sing praises to your name.

2 SAMUEL 22:50

Love is like a bank, the more you put in,
the more your interest grows.

*For I have given you an example, that ye should
do as I have done to you.*

JOHN 13:15 AV

There can be no rainbow unless it has rained.

...your Father...makes his sun rise on the evil and on the good, and sends rain on the righteous and on the unrighteous.

MATTHEW 5:45

The first duty of every Christian is to be sure
he lays no stumbling block in another's way.

*If any of you put a stumbling block before one of these
little ones who believe in me, it would be better for you
if a great millstone were hung around your neck
and you were thrown into the sea.*

MARK 9:42

Some folk are born fools, but the majority
of us become so through practice.

*The mouths of fools are their ruin, and their
lips a snare to themselves.*

PROVERBS 18:7

Calvary restored mankind's lost inheritance.

God so loved the world, that he gave his only begotten Son, that whosoever believeth in him should not perish, but have everlasting life.

JOHN 3:16 AV

The main reason our Lord gives for not worrying about the future is that it's completely in His hands.

Do not let your hearts be troubled...In my Father's house there are many dwelling places. If it were not so, would I have told you that I go to prepare a place for you?

JOHN 14:1A,2

The best way to live in the world
is to live above it.

*If any man love the world, the love of
the Father is not in him.*

1 JOHN 2:15 AV

Your church may point you to Heaven,
but it cannot carry you there.

Who shall ascend into the hill of the Lord? Or who shall
stand in his holy place? He that hath
clean hands, and a pure heart...

PSALM 24:3-4A AV

Failure's other names: wait, tomorrow, too busy, good enough, not my job.

Instead, put on the Lord Jesus Christ, and make no provision for the flesh, to gratify its desires.

ROMANS 13:14

A man knows the least of the
influence of his own life.

...whoever wishes to become great among
you must be your servant.

MARK 10:43

Misunderstanding is the source
of untold sorrows.

...they are to avoid wrangling over words, which does no
good but only ruins those who are listening.

2 TIMOTHY 2:14

Serving Christ under law is a duty,
under love is a delight.

For the love of Christ urges us on.

2 CORINTHIANS 5:14

One life can influence an entire community,
just as a flower can fill a room with
sweet perfume.

*Those who are wise shall shine like the brightness of the
sky, and those who lead many to righteousness,
like the stars for ever and ever.*

DANIEL 12:3

A man may buy a house, but only a
woman can make it a home.

A capable wife...looks well to the ways of her household.

PROVERBS 31:10A,27A

When the OUTLOOK is not good,
try the UPLOOK.

*But filled with the Holy Spirit, (Stephen) gazed into
heaven and saw the glory of God and Jesus
standing at the right hand of God.*

ACTS 7:55

So-called innocent amusements of the world
are only contrivances to forget God.

*When you have eaten your fill, take care
that you do not forget the Lord.*

DEUTERONOMY 6:11B-12A

Of all the things you wear, your expression is the most important.

...you make him glad with the joy of your presence.

PSALM 21:6B

Success lies not in what we start,
but in what we finish.

And let us not be weary in well doing: for in
due season we shall reap, if we faint not.

GALATIANS 6:9 AV

Faith is the vision of the heart.
It sees God in the dark, as in the day.

The just shall live by faith.

ROMANS 1:17B AV

Aim to carve your name on
hearts, not on marble.

*Come and hear, all ye that fear God, and I
will declare what he hath done for my soul.*

PSALM 66:16 AV

Before you tell someone your troubles,
ask yourself, would I listen to theirs?

If one gives answer before hearing, it is folly and shame.

PROVERBS 18:13

Those who are drawn towards Christ are
necessarily drawn towards each other.

*...but if we walk in the light as he himself is in the light,
we have fellowship with one another...*

1 JOHN 1:7

God gives us crosses in this life, so that
we may wear crowns in the next.

*To him that overcometh will I grant to sit with me in my
throne, even as I also overcame, and am set
down with my Father in his throne.*

REVELATION 3:21 AV

Grudges, like babies, grow larger when nursed.

Beloved, do not grumble against one another.

JAMES 5:9A

What you leave IN your children, should be more than what you leave TO them.

Sons are indeed a heritage from the Lord, the fruit of the womb a reward.

PSALM 127:3

To have an upright life, lean on Jesus.

...whoso putteth his trust in the Lord shall be safe.

PROVERBS 29:25B AV

Repentant prayer is one weapon Satan
cannot duplicate.

*I tell you, there is joy in the presence of the angels
of God over one sinner who repents.*

LUKE 15:10

The crowns we cast at Jesus' feet must
all be won on earth.

*For this slight momentary affliction is preparing us for an
eternal weight of glory beyond all measure...*

2 CORINTHIANS 4:17

When we open our heart to Jesus, God
opens our mind to His Word.

*Those who are unspiritual do not receive the gifts of God's
Spirit, for they are foolishness to them, and they are
unable to understand them because they
are spiritually discerned.*

1 CORINTHIANS 2:14

There is but one easy place in this world,
that is the grave. (Beecher)

*Therefore, my beloved, be steadfast, immovable, always
excelling in the work of the Lord, because you know that
in the Lord your labour is not in vain.*

1 CORINTHIANS 15:58

Work that is cheerfully done is
usually well done.

And whatsoever ye do, do it heartily, as to the Lord, and
not unto men...for ye serve the Lord Christ.

COLOSSIANS 3:23-24 AV

The best way to kill time is to
work it to death.

God blessed the seventh day and hallowed it, because on it
God rested from all the work that
he had done in creation.

GENESIS 2:3

The easiest way to keep temptation
from growing is to nip it in the bud.

*Keep awake and pray that you may not come into the
time of trial; the spirit indeed is willing,
but the flesh is weak.*

MARK 14:38

Great faithfulness is exhibited not so much
in ability to do, as to suffer.

*Do not fear what you are about to suffer...Be faithful
until death, and I will give you the crown of life.*

REVELATION 2:10

It is good to follow in the footsteps of a pastor
who follows in the footprints of the Master.

Our steps are made firm by the Lord,
when he delights in our way.

PSALM 37:23

When tempted to lose patience with someone,
stop, think how patient God
has been with you.

Love is patient; love is kind.

1 CORINTHIANS 13:4A

Great results cannot be achieved at once,
but as we walk – step by step.

*...the Lord direct your hearts into the love of God,
and into the patient waiting for Christ.*

2 THESSALONIANS 3:5 AV

Every footstep in life trembles with possibilities; every mile is big with destiny.

My steps have held fast to your paths; my feet have not slipped.

PSALM 17:5

The one base thing in the universe is to receive
favours and render none.

*For where there is envy and selfish ambition, there will
also be disorder...But the wisdom from above is first pure,
then peaceable, gentle, willing to yield, full of mercy and
good fruits, without a trace of partiality or hypocrisy.*

JAMES 3:16-17

Life is a succession of lessons, which
must be lived to be understood.

*Blessed are those who hunger and thirst for
righteousness, for they will be filled.*

MATTHEW 5:6

We gain strength from temptations we resist.

Resist the devil, and he will flee from you.

JAMES 4:7 AV

There is no trait of character more
enriching than simple humility.

*For all who exalt themselves will be humbled, and
those who humble themselves will be exalted.*

LUKE 14:11

The most important thing is not so much where
we stand as the direction in
which we are going.

*Be strong and bold; have no fear or dread...because
it is the Lord your God who goes with you.*

DEUTERONOMY 31:6

To win takes not luck but pluck; not wishbone but backbone.

By your endurance you will gain your souls.

LUKE 21:19

A man is tomorrow what he thinks today.

Set your affection on things above, not on things on the earth.

COLOSSIANS 3:2 AV

Darkness cannot put out the Light; it can only make Him brighter.

The light shines in the darkness, and the darkness did not overcome it.

JOHN 1:5

God made our faces round, only we
can make them long.

*And whenever you fast, do not look dismal, like the
hypocrites, for they disfigure their faces so as to show
others that they are fasting. Truly I tell you,
they have received their reward.*

MATTHEW 6:16

As we grow older, we acquire the
faces we deserve.

A glad heart makes a cheerful countenance.

PROVERBS 15:13

Judging from church attendance, there won't be many men in heaven.

If we say that we have fellowship with him, and walk in darkness, we lie, and do not the truth.

1 JOHN 1:6 AV

Few people get dizzy from doing
too many good turns.

*As God's chosen ones, holy and beloved, clothe
yourselves with compassion, kindness, humility,
meekness, and patience.*

COLOSSIANS 3:12

A sure way to freeze to death is to
be wrapped up in yourself.

*A person's pride will bring humiliation, but one
who is lowly in spirit will obtain honour.*

PROVERBS 29:23

The only way some people get exercise is by throwing bouquets at themselves.

...ungodly sinners...are bombastic in speech, flattering people to their own advantage.

JUDE 15,16

There are two difficult things in life, one is to make a name for yourself, the other to keep it.

A good name is to be chosen rather than great riches, and favour is better than silver or gold.

PROVERBS 22:1

Each one of us should keep a large cemetery to bury the faults of our friends.

Above all, maintain constant love for one another, for love covers a multitude of sins.

1 PETER 4:8

Others will follow your footsteps more easily
than they will follow your advice.

*As Jesus was walking along, he saw a man called
Matthew sitting at the tax booth; and he said to him,
'Follow me'. And he got up and followed him.*

MATTHEW 9:9

When the heart is converted, the
wallet will be inverted.

...the righteous give and do not hold back.

PROVERBS 21:26

Don't give from the top of the purse,
but the bottom of the heart.

For all of them have contributed out of their abundance,
but she out of her poverty has put in
all she had to live on.

LUKE 21:4

God demands a whole heart, but
cradles a broken one.

He heals the brokenhearted, and binds up their wounds.

PSALM 147:3

Being bald has its advantages. When company comes all you have to straighten is your tie.

...the very hairs of your head are all numbered.

MATTHEW 10:30 AV

Enthusiasm is the greatest business
asset in the world.

Do not lag in zeal, be ardent in spirit, serve the Lord.

ROMANS 12:11

Clouds may cover the sunshine, they cannot banish the sun.

The sun shall be no more thy light by day...but the Lord shall be unto thee an everlasting light.

Isaiah 60:19 AV

Courage is the anchor that holds one steady,
and enables one to climb on and on.

Be of good courage, and he shall strengthen your
heart, all ye that hope in the Lord.

PSALM 31:24 AV

Becoming a Christian is letting the
love of God into your heart and soul.

*Listen! I am standing at the door, knocking; if you hear
my voice and open the door, I will come in to you
and eat with you and you with me.*

REVELATION 3:20

A friend is the first person to come
in when others go out.

...a true friend sticks closer than one's nearest kin.

PROVERBS 18:24B

Through the footprints of faith we see
in Jesus everything that God IS.

No one has ever seen God. It is God the only
Son...who has made him known.

JOHN 1:18